Contents

Medicines

A FAMILY MEDICINE CHEST NEEDS TO CONTAIN:

Paracetamol and Ibuprofen
People with stomach
ulcers or asthma should
not take Ibuprofen unless
on medical advice

Dressings

**Paracetamol or Ibuprofen
syrups for children**

Plasters

Rehydration mixture

Digital
Thermometer

Sunscreen factor 15 or higher,
factor 30 for babies or
young children

Medicines

REMEMBER

- Keep the medicine chest in a secure, locked place, out of reach of small children.

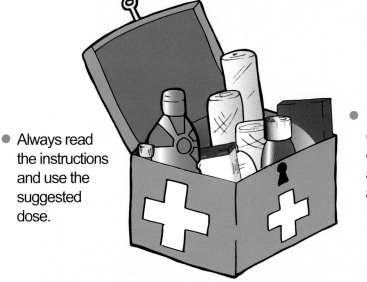

- Always read the instructions and use the suggested dose.

- Use child-proof containers for all medicines and tablets.

- Don't use medicines past their sell-by-date.

- Take all unwanted and out-of-date medicines back to the pharmacy.

- Don`t take anybody else`s prescribed medication.

- Remember the names of medication that your family take regularly.

Temperature

Your child could have a temperature for many reasons.

Normal body temperature is 37°C (98.6°F).

If your child is flushed or feels sweaty with a temperature over 38°C (100.4°F)

HERE'S WHAT TO DO

- Give paracetamol regularly to reduce the temperature but don`t exceed the recommended dose.

- Encourage your child to have more cool drinks.

- Make sure the room is not too warm.

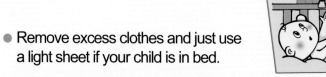

- Remove excess clothes and just use a light sheet if your child is in bed.

Temperature

TAKING YOUR CHILD'S TEMPERATURE

For babies place a digital thermometer under the arm.

For children place a digital thermometer under the tongue.

Leave the thermometer in place for 3 minutes to allow it to register.

Thermometer strips, placed on the forehead, will give an approximate reading, to show if your child's temperature is normal, too hot or too cold.

If your child`s temperature remains high or your child has other symptoms as well, ring NHS direct on 0845 4647 or visit your GP.

Rashes

Rashes can be caused by many different things, most of which are unlikely to be serious.

HOWEVER

If your child has a rash which does not fade when you press a glass tumbler or a finger against it **DIAL 999** immediately.

This is a sign of meningitis which, although rare, could cause death.

REDUCE THE RISK

- Make sure that your child has the Hib and Meningococcus C vaccinations. Both are safe and extremely effective against two types of meningitis.

- Unfortunately, vaccinations are not yet available for all forms of meninigtis, so you still need to be aware of it even if your child has had all their vaccinations.

- If you have any concerns about immunisations seek advice from your GP or health visitor.

Rashes

For any other rashes
HERE`S WHAT TO DO

- Encourage your child to rest and watch closely for signs of illness.

- Give paracetamol if your child is restless.

- Make sure that your child is drinking plenty of fluids.

- Visit your GP or ring NHS Direct on 0845 4647 if the condition gets worse or other symptoms develop.

For nappy rash
HERE`S WHAT TO DO

- Treat the rash with ointment from the pharmacy.
- Don't use talcum powder or wet wipes.
- Use warm water to clean the nappy area.

REDUCE THE RISK

- Change dirty nappies as soon as possible.

Diarrhoea & Vomiting

Upset tummies are not unusual.

However, if your child is also showing other signs of illness or is not responding normally, always ring NHS direct on 0845 4647 or your GP for advice.

Remember - You know your child better than anyone else.

HERE`S WHAT TO DO

General care:

- Breast fed babies - Continue to feed as normal.

- Bottle-fed babies - Give rehydration fluids in small quantities.
  Reintroduce milk gradually.

- For older children - Give sips of rehydration fluid at first.
  Gradually increase the amount of liquids.
  Avoid milk for 24 hours.
  After about 8 hours start with a very bland diet e.g. toast.
  Avoid fatty or spicy foods.

Diarrhoea & Vomiting

Call your GP or NHS Direct if your child:

- Has been vomiting or had diarrhoea for more than one day.

- Also has a fever.

- Has blood in their diarrhoea or vomit.

REDUCE THE RISK

- Store chilled food correctly.

- Always wash hands after using the toilet and before eating or preparing food.

- Keep kitchen surfaces clean, especially after handling raw meat.

- Ensure that all food is cooked thoroughly.

- If reheating food, always ensure that it is piping hot.

- Clean up thoroughly after someone in the family has been ill.

Falls

Children often fall over. Most falls are not a problem, but if your child has a bad fall

HERE`S WHAT TO DO

DIAL 999 if your child:

- Has injured their neck or back.
  DO NOT MOVE YOUR CHILD

- Is unconscious. If you are certain that there is no possibility of a neck or back injury, put your child in the recovery position as shown.

- Has a fit or convulsion after a fall.

Call NHS direct on 0845 4647 or visit Accident & Emergency (A&E) if your child is:

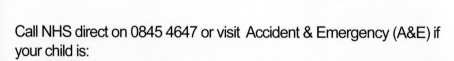

- Finding it difficult to move part of their body as they may have a broken bone.

- Dazed, groggy, vomiting or has hearing or vision difficulties.

Falls

If your child has any bang to the head watch them very closely for the next 48 hours.

REDUCE THE RISK

- Don't leave things anywhere that they can be tripped over.

- Fit safety catches to opening windows.

- Use stair gates.

- Teach toddlers how to use the stairs safely.

- Teach children only to play in safe areas.

Bleeding

HERE`S WHAT TO DO

For **serious cuts**

- Press on the wound with a clean cloth or bandage to stop the flow of blood.

- DO NOT REMOVE anything sticking out of the wound.

Accident and Emergency

- Take your child to A&E.

For **minor cuts**

- Clean with tap water.

- Cover with a plaster or dry bandage.

Bleeding

For **nose bleeds**

- Sit your child down with their head bent forward.

- Pinch the soft part of the nose until the bleeding stops.

- If the nose is still bleeding after 20 minutes ring your GP or NHS Direct on 0845 4647.

REDUCE THE RISK

- Keep sharp objects out of the reach of young children.

- Discuss with your children the safest thing to do if they see something like broken glass or a needle/syringe.

Choking

If your child is choking on something
HERE`S WHAT TO DO

- **DIAL 999** if your child's lips are tinged blue or they are having difficulty breathing.

- **DO NOT** stick your fingers down their throat to remove the object.

- **DO** encourage your child to try and cough the object out.

- **DO** bend your child over and slap their back between the shoulder blades to try and dislodge the object. Give up to five back slaps.

For babies lay them down the length of your arm and use the heel of your hand to give five smart blows between the shoulder blades.

Choking

If this hasn`t worked you will need to try chest thrusts:

- Place your arms around your child, just below the ribs, and squeeze firmly upwards five times with the heel of your hand.

  For babies use only two fingers, not the heel of your hand, so as not to damage their delicate internal organs.

  For children over eight years old, place your fist on the child`s tummy, put your other hand over your fist, then pull inwards and upwards five times.

- Repeat cycles of five back slaps and five chest thrusts.

REDUCE THE RISK

- Keep small objects well out of the reach of small children who will put them in their mouth.

- Do not give small children whole nuts or hard sweets.

- Sit down to eat.

Breathing Difficulties

Breathing difficulties in children should never be ignored.

HERE`S WHAT TO DO

- **DIAL 999** if your child's lips are tinged blue or they are having difficulty speaking.

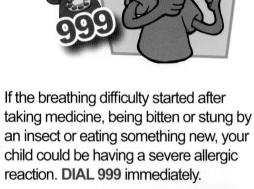

- If the breathing difficulty started after taking medicine, being bitten or stung by an insect or eating something new, your child could be having a severe allergic reaction. **DIAL 999** immediately.

- If your child is wheezing they may have asthma. Visit your GP or call NHS Direct on 0845 4647 for advice.

Breathing Difficulties

REDUCE THE RISK

- If your child has severe allergic reactions make sure that anyone looking after them knows about the problem and what to avoid.

Notes for baby sitter

Caroline's allergies

Nuts
Bee stings

Caroline also has asthma

Her inhaler is in the bathroom cabinet.

- If your child has asthma make sure that their inhaler is used as prescribed and ensure that you don't run out of medication.

- Ensure that your children DO NOT eat, sleep or play in a smoky environment.

Second-hand smoke can lead to heart disease and lung cancer and can make illnesses like asthma worse.

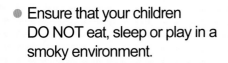

Accidental Poisoning

The main causes of accidental poisoning are from mistaking medicines and chemicals for sweets and drinks.

HERE`S WHAT TO DO

- **DIAL 999** if your child is drowsy, unconscious or not able to breathe properly.

- Call NHS Direct on 0845 4647 if your child has swallowed something that they shouldn`t have, even if they seem okay.

- DO NOT try to make your child sick.

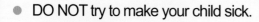

- If you go to the hospital remember to take the container of poison with you.

Accidental Poisoning

REDUCE THE RISK

- Lock all medicines and chemicals out of sight and reach of children.

- Keep all products in their original containers.

- Do not store medicines or cleaning products near food.

- Never take or give medicine in the dark.

- Buy products that have child resistant caps.

- Make sure that you don't have any poisonous plants or berries in the garden.

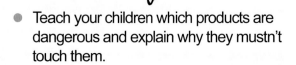

- Teach your children which products are dangerous and explain why they mustn't touch them.

21

Fires, Burns & Scalds

If your child has been in a fire or has had an electric shock **DIAL 999.**

For other burns and scalds
HERE`S WHAT TO DO

- Take off any rings, bracelets, necklaces or shoes that could restrict blood flow.

- Cool the affected area under cool running water for 15 minutes.

- DO NOT apply any creams or ointments.

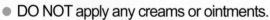

- Cover with cling film or a clean, non-fluffy cloth such as a tea-towel or handkerchief.

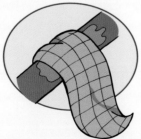

- Do not burst any blisters. Call NHS Direct on 0845 4647 for advice if the burnt area is blistered.

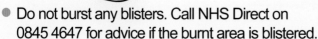

Fires, Burns & Scalds

If the burnt area is larger than the size of your child's hand or if it is on the face visit A&E or call NHS Direct on 0845 4647.

REDUCE THE RISK

- Don't let your children do jobs involving hot objects or liquids.

- Always supervise children near hot things.

- Don't let the kettle cable dangle.

- Use the back rings and turn panhandles away from the edge.

- Never leave a hot iron.

- Use fireguards.

- Take care with candles.

- When filling the bath run the cold water first and never leave the hot tap running.

- Don't use electrical appliances in the bathroom.

- Use high protection sun cream.

- Check smoke alarms regularly.

- Discuss a fire escape plan with your children.

Drowning

Small children can drown in just a few centimetres of water.

If your child is drowning
HERE`S WHAT TO DO

- Remove your child from the water.

- **DIAL 999.**

- If your child is not breathing, you will need to do mouth to mouth resuscitation. Tell the controller when you **DIAL 999** and they will talk you through how to do this.

- If your child is breathing put them in the recovery position, as shown, so that they do not choke on any vomit.

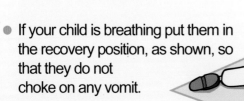

Drowning

REDUCE THE RISK

- Never leave babies or small children alone in the bath.

- Always watch your children carefully when they are playing in or near water.

- Teach your children how to swim.

- Teach your children about the dangers of ponds, lakes, rivers, canals and seas.

Head Lice

- Head lice are tiny insects that live on the head close to the skin.

- Head lice lay eggs, which they glue to the hair.

- Nits are the empty eggshells left in the hair.

- Head lice are difficult to see because they are tiny.

- Remember, head lice like clean hair as well as dirty hair.

Actual size

If your child has head lice

HERE`S WHAT TO DO

The Wet Combing Method

- Wash the hair.

- Apply lots of conditioner.

- Separate the hair into tiny sections.

- Comb from the roots to the end of each section with a nit comb.

- Work methodically over the whole head for at least 30 minutes.

- Rinse as normal.

- Repeat every other day for at least two weeks.

NIT COMB 3000

Head Lice

Medicated Lotion or Rinse

- Chemical treatments to kill head lice are available from your pharmacist or health visitor who will explain how to use them.

- Care should be taken when applying these treatments because they are usually toxic.

- Babies, pregnant women or people with asthma should not use these treatments without their doctor's advice.

REDUCE THE RISK

- Comb your child's hair twice a day.

- Check your child's head for lice or eggs every week paying particular attention to the neckline, behind the ears and the top of the head.

- Keep long hair tied up for school.

If anyone in your family catches head lice everybody else's hair needs checking as well.

Threadworms

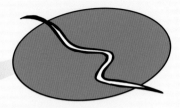

Threadworms are tiny white thread-like worms that cause intense itching of the bottom, especially at night.
They can sometimes be seen in poo.

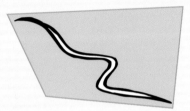

Threadworm eggs can survive outside the body and are easily passed to other people if strict standards of hygiene are not followed.

If your child gets worms
HERE`S WHAT TO DO

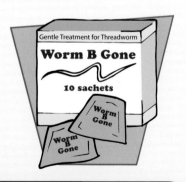

- Treat your child AND everyone else in the family with special medicine that is available from your pharmacist or GP.

Gentle Treatment for Threadworm
Worm B Gone
10 sachets
Worm B Gone
Worm B Gone

Women who are pregnant or breastfeeding should NOT use these medicines; they need to ask their GP for advice.

Threadworms

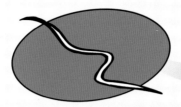

- Follow these strict standards of hygiene for at least two weeks after taking the medicine to stop re-infestation:

- Wash hands thoroughly and scrub nails after visiting the toilet and before eating.

- Keep fingernails short.

- Make sure everyone in the family has their own towel.

- Give your child close fitting pants to wear at night to stop them scratching their bottom when they are asleep.

- Wash around your child's bottom every morning.

- Change and wash your child's nightwear every day.

REDUCE THE RISK

- Make sure that your children always wash their hands after using the toilet and before eating.

- Encourage your children to stop thumb sucking and nail biting.

What to do in an emergency

- STAY CALM.

- **DIAL 999** and give details of the situation clearly.

- Do not give the injured or sick person anything to eat, drink or smoke.

- Do not stick anything in their mouth.

- Do not move the person if they may have injured their back/neck.

- If you need to go to hospital with one of your children remember to arrange care for any other children or take them with you if this is not possible.
Do not leave children at home alone.

Contacts

Useful contacts for help and advice:

NHS Direct   **tel: 0845 4647**   www.nhsdirect.nhs.uk
(England & Wales)   www.nhsdirect.wales.nhs.uk

NHS24 (Scotland)   **tel: 08454 24 24 24**   www.nhs24.com

Child Accident Prevention Trust (CAPT)
tel: 020 7608 3828
www.capt.org.uk

Royal Society for the Prevention of Accidents (RoSPA)
tel: 0121 248 2000
www.rospa.com

British Red Cross
tel: 0844 871 8000
www.redcross.org.uk/what-we-do/first-aid

St.John Ambulance
tel: 0870 010 4950
www.sja.org.uk

Your Local Fire Service can be contacted for advice on fire prevention. All fire brigades will provide FREE home safety checks.

Your local health visitor can be contacted via your GP practice.

Add your GP's number here

Other numbers in your area:

Caring for Kids - Book 6

Family First Aid is an essential, easy to follow guide for all parents and carers. It gives clear advice, presented in easy to follow cartoons, on how to deal with a wide range of childhood illnesses and accidents.

 Medicine Chest

 Temperature

 Rashes

 Diarrhoea & Vomiting

 Falls

 Bleeding

 Choking

 Fires, Burns & Scalds

 Breathing Difficulties

 Accidental Poisoning

 Drowning

 Head Lice

 Threadworms

 What to do in an emergency

Family First Aid is part of the Caring For Kids series.
Also available:

ISBN 978-1-906036-45-4

9 781906 036454

www.**kidpremiership**.com

t 01484 668008   f 01484 668009   e mail@kidpremiership.com

One17ED, The Dyehouse, Armitage Bridge, Huddersfield, HD4 7PD